MAR 0 8 2012

D1376999

FIRST NATIONS OF NORTH AMERICA

SOUTHWEST INDIANS

MELISSA McDANIEL

HEINEMANN LIBRARY
CHICAGO, ILLINOIS

NORTH PALM BEACH PUBLIC LIBRARY

www.heinemannraintree.com
Visit our website to find out more information about Heinemann-Raintree books.

To order:
☎ Phone 888-454-2279
💻 Visit www.heinemannraintree.com to browse our catalog and order online.

© 2012 Heinemann Library
an imprint of Capstone Global Library, LLC
Chicago, Illinois

All rights reserved. No part of this publication may be reproduced or transmitted in any form or by any means, electronic or mechanical, including photocopying, recording, taping, or any information storage and retrieval system, without permission in writing from the publisher.

Original illustrations © Capstone Global Library, Ltd.
Illustrated by Mapping Specialists, Ltd.
Originated by Capstone Global Library, Ltd.
Printed in China by China Translation and Printing Services

14 13 12 11
10 9 8 7 6 5 4 3 2 1

Library of Congress Cataloging-in-Publication Data
McDaniel, Melissa, 1964-
  Southwest Indians / Melissa McDaniel.
    p. cm.—(First nations of North America)
  Includes bibliographical references and index.
  ISBN 978-1-4329-4953-2 (hc)—ISBN 978-1-4329-4964-8
(pb) 1. Indians of North America—Southwest, New—Juvenile
literature. I. Title.
  E78.S7M1357 2012
  979.004'97—dc22   2010040616

Acknowledgements

The author and publisher are grateful to the following for permission to reproduce copyright material: Corbis: pp. 14 (© Werner Forman), 15 (© Pete Saloutos), 27 (© Corbis), 41 (© Tom Bean); Getty Images: pp. 5 (David W. Hamilton), 25 (Buyenlarge), 26 (Keystone), 29 (Richard Ross), 32 (MPI), 38 (Time & Life Pictures), 39 (Fotosearch), 40 (TIM SLOAN/AFP); Library of Congress Prints and Photographs Division: pp. 4, 11, 16, 18, 21, 23, 24; National Geographic Stock: pp. 19 (CHARLES MARTIN), 33 (W. LANGDON KIHN); Nativestock.com: pp. 22 (© Marilyn Angel Wynn), 30 (© Marilyn Angel Wynn), 31 (© Marilyn Angel Wynn), 35 (© Marilyn Angel Wynn), 37 (© Marilyn Angel Wynn); Photolibrary: pp. 10 (© Regien Paassen), 13 (© Caitlin Mirra), 17 (© Jonathan A Meyers), 20 (© Jim Feliciano), 34 (© Paul B. Moore); The Granger Collection, NYC: p. 36.

Cover photograph of Navajo etched pottery vase made from clay reproduced with permission from Nativestock.com (© Marilyn Angel Wynn).

We would like to thank Dr. Scott Stevens for his invaluable help in the preparation of this book.

Every effort has been made to contact copyright holders of any material reproduced in this book. Any omissions will be rectified in subsequent printings if notice is given to the publisher.

All the Internet addresses (URLs) given in this book were valid at the time of going to press. However, due to the dynamic nature of the Internet, some addresses may have changed, or sites may have changed or ceased to exist since publication. While the author and publisher regret any inconvenience this may cause readers, no responsibility for any such changes can be accepted by either the author or the publisher.

Contents

Some words are shown in bold **like this**. You can find out what they mean by looking in the glossary.

Who Were the First People in North America?

On a dusty clifftop in northern Arizona sits a village called Oraibi. Hopi people have been living in Oraibi for about 900 years. This makes Oraibi one of the oldest settlements in what is now the United States. The Hopi people are American Indians. American Indians have been building towns in the Southwest since before Europeans first arrived on the continent.

American Indians are the **descendants** of the first people to arrive in North America. Today American Indians live in all parts of North America. Many of them keep up the traditions and **customs** of their **ancestors**.

▲ American Indians have lived in the Southwest for thousands of years.

◀ Many American Indians follow the traditions of their ancestors.

Different groups of American Indians have different customs. This book will discuss the customs, beliefs, ways of life, and history of the peoples from the Southwest region of North America.

American Indian or Native American?

When explorer Christopher Columbus sailed across the Atlantic Ocean in 1492 and reached North America, he thought he had reached the Indies, a region in Asia. He called the people who lived there "Indians."

Today, the descendants of the first peoples in North America are most often called American Indians or Native Americans. There is no agreement as to which term is correct. The word "native" can describe something or someone that did not move from somewhere else. Most of these people today, however, prefer to be referred to by their **tribe** or **nation affiliation**, such as Pueblo or Zuni.

The first people in North America

The first people arrived in North America more than 12,000 years ago. Scientists believe they came from Asia. At the time, Earth was colder than it is today, and more of the world's water was frozen into ice. Because of this, sea levels were lower. A wide section of land rose above the water in the **Bering Strait**, which today separates Russia from Alaska. People from Asia simply walked across this section of land to North America.

These early first people of North America were hunters. In their search for large **game**, they gradually spread across North America.

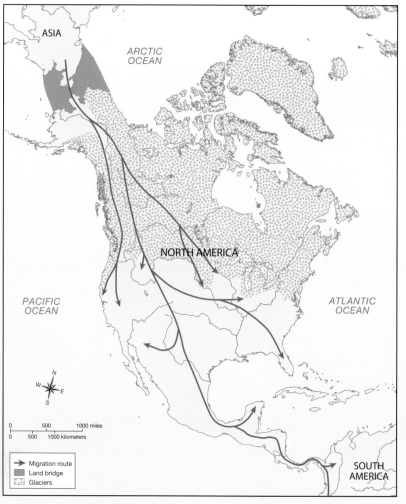

◄ This map shows the routes the first people to arrive in North America took.

These first people settled into different parts of North America. In these different regions, they developed different **traits** and ways of life. Since these first people were different from each other, people who study **traditional** American Indian cultures divide the continent into different cultural regions.

The southwestern cultural region includes Arizona and New Mexico. It also includes southern Utah, southwestern Colorado, and West Texas. Native peoples of northern Mexico are also part of this cultural region.

◄ This map shows how regions where American Indians with similar cultures and lifestyles lived.

Many nations

The peoples of the Southwest settled into many different nations. Each of these **nations** has its own culture.

The major nations in the Southwest include:

Navajo: The Navajo people are called the Diné in their own language. They are largest American Indian nation in the United States today. Many Navajos raise sheep. They are known for weaving beautiful wool blankets.

Apache: Apaches were traditionally hunters, famed for their skill on horseback. They ranged across much of the Southwest in their search for game.

Pueblo: The Pueblo people built cities made of rock and **adobe** in northern New Mexico. The word pueblo means "town" in Spanish, and it refers to both the Pueblo people and the towns they live in. The Pueblo group includes many different nations and towns, including Acoma, Taos, Laguna, Picuris, and Jemez.

Hopi: The Hopi people are sometimes considered part of the Pueblo group because they live in pueblos. Their towns are in northern Arizona. Today, Hopis are considered among the most traditional of American Indians.

Zuni: The Zuni people live in pueblos in western New Mexico. Their language is not related to that of any other Pueblo people.

Tohono O'odham: The Tohono O'odham live in the desert of southern Arizona. In the past, they gathered much of their food from desert plants.

Akimel O'odham: The Akimel O'odham traditionally lived along rivers in southern Arizona. Water from the rivers helped them to grow crops.

Upland Yumans: This group consists of three nations—the Havasupai, the Hualapai, and the Yavapai. They live in the canyons of northern Arizona.

River Yumans: The Mohave, the Yuma, and other nations traditionally farmed along the Colorado River in southern Arizona.

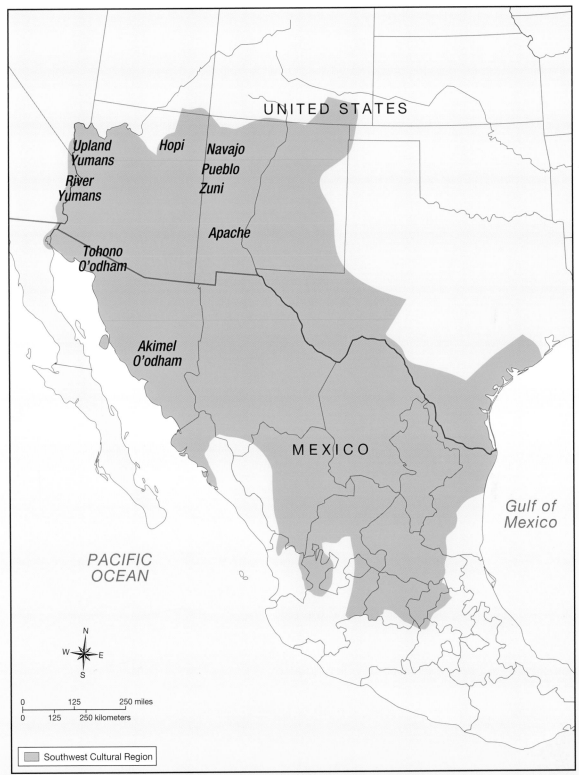

UNITED STATES

Upland Yumans

Hopi

Navajo
Pueblo
Zuni

River Yumans

Apache

Tohono O'odham

Akimel O'odham

MEXICO

PACIFIC OCEAN

Gulf of Mexico

N
W E
S

0   125   250 miles
0   125   250 kilometers

◻ Southwest Cultural Region

▲ This map shows where the major Indian nations of the Southwest were located.

What Is Land in the Southwest Like?

The Southwest is a magnificent but harsh land. Much of it is rocky desert dotted with cacti. Other regions boast spectacular canyons, vast empty flatlands, and towering mountains covered with pine trees.

Most of the Southwest is dry. It averages just 4 to 20 inches (10 to 50 centimeters) of rain each year. Most of the rain comes in the summer. Summers are extremely hot. In southern Arizona, the temperature usually tops 100°F (38°C) for three months each year. Winters are cold. Even in the desert, the temperature often drops below freezing.

▲ Dramatic red spires are sprinkled throughout Monument Valley. This park is part of the Navajo **Reservation**.

In the past, Southwest Indians had to be very knowledgeable about their surroundings to survive. Water was precious. Native towns clustered near rivers. In areas without rivers, people knew every water source, and they made good use of the water that fell from the sky.

Farming in the Southwest

Despite the dry land, Indians throughout the Southwest farmed. They knew exactly when to plant certain crops. They knew when the hard summer rains would come, and where the water would drain. They could use that water for their crops.

Many early Southwest Indians moved with the seasons, following food sources. Year after year, they would return to certain spots to gather food.

Horses helped some people survive in the Southwest. Apaches hunted on horseback. This allowed them to travel farther across the land, searching for **game**.

▶ Less than 12 inches (30 centimeters) of rain falls each year on the Hopis' land, yet they grew corn, beans, squash, sunflowers, melons, and much more.

11

Who Were the First Southwest Indians?

The first people to enter the Southwest were hunters. They used spears to hunt large animals such as bison and **mammoths**. The people moved from place to place following **game**. They found shelter in caves or under rock overhangs.

Over time, the Southwest became hotter and drier. Most of the large animals disappeared. People hunted smaller animals and gathered nuts and seeds. They eventually began farming, which provided them with a steady supply of food.

Three rich cultures arose in the Southwest around 2,000 years ago—the Mogollon, the Hohokam, and the Ancestral Pueblo, who are sometimes called the Anasazi.

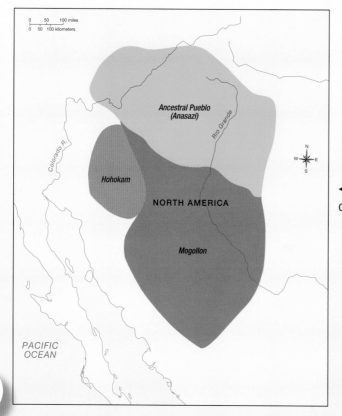

◄ This map shows where the earliest peoples of the Southwest lived.

Where the first people lived

The Mogollon people lived in what is now eastern Arizona and western New Mexico. The Mogollons were the first farmers in the Southwest. They grew corn, squash, and beans. They also made fine pottery. The Hohokam people lived in the southern Arizona desert. They built hundreds of miles of canals to bring water from the Salt and Gila rivers to irrigate their crops.

Ancestral Puebloans settled in the **Four Corners** region. This is the region where the perfectly square corners of Arizona, New Mexico, Colorado, and Utah meet. The Ancestral Puebloans built large cities. Sometimes they carved buildings into cliff walls. Other times they made buildings out of stone.

The largest Ancestral Puebloan city was in Chaco Canyon, in what is now northwestern New Mexico. Grand roads 30 feet (9 meters) wide extended out from Chaco Canyon like the spokes on a bicycle wheel. These roads connected Chaco to distant, smaller towns.

◄ Pueblo Bonito ("Pretty Village" in Spanish) was the biggest building in Chaco Canyon. A million large stone blocks were used to build its more than 600 rooms.

13

Mimbres Pottery

What can you learn from a pot? **Archaeologists** learn much by studying the unique pottery of the Mimbres people, a group belonging to the Mogollon culture. Archaeologists determined that women made the pottery, because pottery tools have been found in the graves of women, but not men. Pots themselves were also buried in graves. Each buried pot, which was put over a dead person's head, had a hole in it. Some people have suggested that these holes were made so that a person's spirit could escape his or her body.

▲ This Mimbres pot has a hole for the spirit to escape.

What happened to the ancient peoples?

Each of these complex cultures grew and developed for centuries. But each also eventually disappeared.

The Mogollon may have eventually joined Ancestral Puebloan villages. The Hohokam began leaving their settlements in the 1300s. Some may have moved to what is now Mexico. Others are probably the **ancestors** of the Tohono O'odham and Akimel O'odham peoples.

In the 1200s, the Ancestral Puebloans began abandoning their cities. No one is sure why. One theory is that many years of **drought** may have forced them to move. The Ancestral Puebloans headed south and settled in new villages.

Navajos and Apaches arrive

The Navajo and Apache peoples were originally from what is now Canada. About 1,000 years ago, they began moving south. They likely began arriving in the Southwest in the 1300s.

Navajos settled in the northern part of the region, near the Puebloan peoples. They began farming and raising sheep after the 1600s.

Apaches continued farther south. They were **nomadic**, moving from place to place in search of game.

▲ The Navajo people began keeping sheep after they settled near the Pueblos. The Pueblos taught them to weave.

What Were Early Southwest Indian Communities Like?

In the early Southwest, Indian **nations** were **traditionally** organized in many different ways. For example, among the Akimel O'odham each village had a leader. The leader was in charge of planning farming projects. The leader also made sure the village was well defended if it was attacked. Village leaders elected an overall leader of the Akimel O'odham nation. He led meetings of the village leaders. The Tohono O'odham also had village leaders, but the nation had no overall leader.

◄ Hopi leaders were always important religious figures, such as this one.

In the past, the Apaches were divided into six different groups, including the Chiricahua and the Mescalero. Rather than having one leader, each group was led by a small group of families.

The Hopi nation is made up of many different villages. Hopi people identify closely with their own village. Their own village is much more important to them than the Hopi nation as a whole.

Languages of the Southwest

Southwest Indians spoke many different languages. The Navajo and Apache languages are related. They both come from a family of languages called Athabascan. The Yuman peoples also speak languages that are related to one another.

Languages spoken by Hopis, Tohono O'odhams, and some Pueblo peoples are related to that spoken by the Aztecs, a powerful nation that dominated central Mexico in the 1400s before the Europeans arrived. This group of languages is called the Uto-Aztecan. Other Puebloan peoples speak the Keresan language. Zunis speak a language all their own. It is not related to any other language spoken in the Southwest.

▲ A Zuni dancer is shown here. About 6,000 people speak the Zuni language.

17

Early Southwest Indian families

Many Southwest Indian nations are divided into groups of families called clans. When two Navajos marry, for example, the husband joins the wife's clan. When children are born, they become members of their mother's clan.

In the past, when two Zunis married, the husband moved in with his new wife's family. Women owned most property in some Southwest Indian nations. Among the Hopi people, farm fields are passed down from mother to child. Navajo women traditionally owned their family's land and livestock. Men owned their own horses and whatever goods they brought to the marriage.

Southwest Indians taught their children life skills at a young age. Girls learned to cook and make pots. Boys learned to hunt. Everyone learned to do their part in planting and harvesting crops.

▲ In many early Southwest Indian societies, both parents traditionally took care of the children. Grandparents, aunts, uncles, and other family members were also involved.

A Day in the Life of an Early Southwest Indian Child

You wake up in the cozy darkness of your home, a wooden house called a **hogan**. You lay still and listen to the soft breathing of your parents and your brothers. You look toward the door and see the orange glow of the Sun just appearing.

You pick up a basket and head to your family fields, where you pick corn, squash, and beans. Later, you will grind corn and help your mother make a stew.

Next, you clean the wool recently cut from your family's sheep. It needs to be cleaned and combed before your mother can spin it into thread. You also collect cedar bark and the fruit of the prickly pear cactus, which your mother uses to dye the wool. Your aunt is teaching you to weave.

You do many jobs during the day, but you also get to play. Your dolls come alive. You race your brother down a **gully** and up the other side. At the end of the long day, you enter the hogan, ready for sleep.

What Was Everyday Life Like for Early Southwest Indians?

The early peoples of the Southwest built many kinds of **traditional** houses. Pueblo people made the largest buildings. They sometimes built apartment buildings that were six stories high. People climbed up ladders to reach the higher stories. These buildings were clustered together into towns.

Pueblo buildings did not have doors or windows on the ground floor. This made the town easier to defend if it was attacked. Pueblos would simply pull up the ladders, so the attackers could not get in.

Some Pueblos made their houses out of stones. They used a mud-based **mortar** to hold the stones together. Some Pueblos also used **adobe** to make their buildings. They made adobe bricks of mud, clay, and straw. The bricks dried in the Sun until they were hard and strong.

▶ Taos Pueblo is the best **preserved pueblo** in the Southwest.

Other types of homes

Navajos lived in round houses called **hogans**. To build a hogan, a framework of logs is covered with bark or mud. The door to the hogan always faces east, to greet the rising Sun.

Apaches moved often in their search for food. They made their shelters quickly. Their houses, called **wickiups**, were like hogans, but they were smaller and lighter. To make a wickiup, Apaches bent thin branches into a dome shape. They then covered the dome with brush and grass.

The Akimel O'odham and Tohono O'odham peoples built small, round houses out of poles. Their flat tops were covered with grass. In the summer, they made simple buildings called ramadas. Most ramadas had no walls, but their roofs provided shelter from the Sun.

▲ Navajos built hogans using bark and mud.

Clothing

Today, Southwest Indians dress the same as non-Indians. They wear jeans and T-shirts, business suits, and cowboy boots. In the past, however, their clothing was different.

Southwest Indians who lived in the desert wore few clothes. Many wore only shorts or skirts made of bark or deerskin. The Tohono O'odham made simple skirts from cotton. In colder weather, they would add robes made from rabbit skins. They usually wore leather sandals.

In parts of the Southwest where the weather was more varied, people wore different kinds of clothes. Pueblo men wore skirts similar to **kilts** and leather sandals. Women wore cotton dresses and sandals or moccasins. For warmth, they would cover themselves with blankets made from deer or rabbit skin.

Navajo women wore simple knitted dresses. Navajo men wore long cotton shirts and knitted leggings. Hunting played a larger role in Apache life, so the Apache had many animal skins. Their shirts, skirts, and leggings were usually made of deerskin.

▲ This Zuni woman is wearing traditional dress.

Hairstyles

Early Navajo people tied their hair behind their head in a large, elaborate knot. Both men and women used this style. Pueblo people also wore their hair in a knot.

Sometimes, traditional hairstyles changed as a person got older. When Hopi girls were old enough to get married, they began twisting their hair into large swirls on either side of their head. This is known as the squash blossom style. After they married, they wore their hair down or in braids.

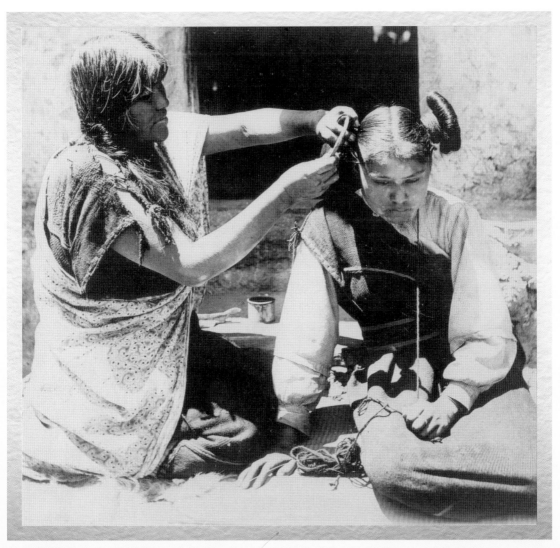

▲ To make the squash blossom hairstyle, a Hopi mother wound her daughter's hair back and forth around a curved piece of wood.

Food for early Southwest Indians

In the dry lands of the Southwest, food was more difficult to find than in some other parts of North America. People in the Southwest gathered wild fruit, nuts, seeds, and other edible plant parts. In the desert, food was especially scarce. The people who lived there went wherever fruit was ripening. The fruit of the saguaro cactus was especially important to them. They ate it fresh, turned it into jam, or dried it and ground it into powder.

Most peoples in the Southwest farmed. Even desert people used what little water there was to grow corn, squash, pumpkins, cotton, and more.

The Hopi and Pueblo peoples were outstanding farmers. Hopis carefully caught rainwater and found underground **springs** to water their fields. Corn was their most important crop. They prepared it in more than 50 different ways!

◄ Tohono O'odham women used a long pole to knock the fruit from the arms of the towering saguaro cactus.

Some people in the Southwest also raised animals. Navajos raised sheep, which they used for both meat and wool. The Pueblo and desert peoples kept turkeys.

Hunting was an important source of food for Southwest Indians. The most common **game** was rabbit. The Havasupai people would have large group hunts. Men, women, boys, and girls could gather and pound on the ground to drive the rabbits out from their hiding places in the underbrush.

In some parts of the region, Southwest Indians hunted deer, antelope, and mountain lions. Apaches who lived east hunted bison.

▲ Apaches hunted deer, antelope, bison, bighorn sheep, and many smaller animals.

25

NORTH PALM BEACH PUBLIC LIBRARY

What Objects Did Early Southwest Indians Make?

Traditional objects made by early Southwest Indians are both useful and beautiful. Pueblo people are known for their pottery. Each village has its own particular style. Acoma pots are very thin. Acoma potters often create dazzling patterns by painting many thin black lines right next to each other. Potters at Santa Clara Pueblo usually carve designs into their pots.

Blankets, jewelry, and baskets

Navajos are famed for their woven wool blankets. The wool is colored with natural dyes made from plants. Navajo blankets have strong designs, often featuring zigzags and diamonds.

▲ Maria Martinez of San Idelfonso Pueblo was one of the greatest Pueblo potters. She made shiny black pots decorated with black designs.

Navajos make stunning jewelry. They make big, bold bracelets, belts, and buckles out of silver. It is often decorated with a blue stone called turquoise.

Southwest Indians have been making baskets for thousands of years. They traditionally used baskets to store food and other goods. The Tohono O'odham weave some baskets so tightly that they can hold water. Today, they sometimes weave animal shapes or maze patterns into their baskets. Apaches make an unusual kind of basket called a burden basket.

▶ Apaches used burden baskets to carry food, firewood, and many other goods.

BIOGRAPHY

Maria Martinez: Pueblo Potter

In Pueblo communities, skills are passed down through families. Maria Martinez, who was born in San Ildefonso Pueblo in 1887, learned pottery from her aunt. She worked hard perfecting her craft and began showing her pots in competitions. Martinez made shiny black pots painted with black designs. These pots earned great praise and helped Pueblo pottery become admired around the world. Martinez died in 1980, but members of her family are still making black-on-black pottery.

What Did Early Southwest Indians Believe?

Each group of Southwest Indians has its own religion, but they all have some things in common. People believe that powerful spirits affect human life. These spirits are everywhere in nature.

Kivas

Pueblo and Hopi peoples hold ceremonies in underground rooms called **kivas**. They build kivas underground because it is said that their **ancestors** originally come up from the center of the Earth.

STORIES AND LEGENDS

Up From the Earth

This is one of many stories Hopi people tell about how their people were created.

Long ago, the ancestors of humans lived beneath the Earth. The people slowly moved through three cave worlds underground. Finally, Spider put a reed through the top of the third cave. The people climbed through the reed into this, the fourth world. They found themselves in the Grand Canyon. The land was dark and covered with water. Spider spun a ball of thread to make the Moon. A bleached deerskin became the Sun. Coyote opened a jar of sparks and they flew into the sky to become stars. Vulture beat his winds and the water withdrew, cutting valleys into the land. The people followed these valleys until they arrived at the highlands where they would make their homes.

In the past, kivas were always round, but today they are sometimes square. To enter a kiva, a person climbs down a ladder through a hole in the roof. There is usually a fire pit in the center and benches around the walls. Typically, only men take part in ceremonies held in kivas.

▲ Some kivas serve only one family, while others are large enough to hold hundreds of people.

Ceremonies

Southwest Indian religious leaders lead the rituals and ceremonies. Many of the religious rituals feature music and dance. Ritual chants and dances are said to help bring good fortune. People might take part in a ceremonial dance to bring rain or a good harvest.

Many groups have healing rituals. These rituals are meant to help sick people become healthy. Some healing rituals are dances. Navajos use sand painting as a healing ritual. To make a sand painting, a shaman sings a chant while carefully pouring colored sand through his fingers to make a picture. The patient then sits on the painting so that the sand can absorb the illness. At the end of the ritual, the sand painting is destroyed.

Kachinas

The Hopi and Pueblo religions feature spirits called **kachinas**. These religions include hundreds of different kachinas. In religious ceremonies, dancers are filled with the spirit of kachinas. Major ceremonies sometimes feature 30 different kachina dancers.

▲ Hopi kachina dolls are often painted with bright colors.

A kachina dancer wears a mask that represents the kachina. Among the Hopi people, the kachina Nataska is shown with a long snout. He carries a bow and knife. Nataska is a frightening figure who helps teach children good behavior. Only men are kachina dancers, even if the kachina figures are female.

Carved wooden dolls that represent the spirits are also called kachinas. These dolls are given to children as gifts.

Religion today

Today some Southwest Indians continue to practice their **traditional** religion. Others are Christian or practice a mix of Christianity and their traditional religion.

▲ Navajo children perform the traditional rainbow dance.

What Happened When the Spanish Arrived?

After Columbus's journey in 1492, the Spanish slowly spread across much of North America and South America. In 1521 Spain conquered the Aztecs, a powerful **nation**. The Spanish soon **plundered** Mexico for its gold and other valuable metals. They shipped these riches back to Europe.

The Spanish heard tales of even greater riches to the north. There, some people said, lay Cibola, seven cities made of gold. The Spanish began sending out **expeditions** to search for these legendary cities. In 1540 a Spanish official named Francisco Vásquez de Coronado headed north with more than 1,000 Spaniards, American Indians, and enslaved Africans. They found no gold.

▲ Coronado's journey across the Southwest lasted more than two years and covered thousands of miles.

In 1582 a Spaniard named Antonio de Espejo discovered that there was silver in what is now northern Arizona. Spanish officials once again began looking north.

Troubled times

In 1598 a wealthy Spanish businessman named Juan de Oñate led soldiers, families, and priests—several hundred people in all—into the land of the Pueblo people to establish a settlement. The newcomers were not friendly toward the Pueblo people. They demanded food and shelter. They forced the Southwest Indians to work for them.

The people of Acoma Pueblo fought back. They attacked some Spanish settlers. Oñate responded with ferocious violence. The Spanish killed more than 800 Acomas. They took children away from their families and put them under the care of Spanish priests.

▲ The Spanish conquered Pueblo towns.

The Pueblo revolt

The Spanish also forced the Pueblo people to become Christian. They whipped or killed people who practiced their own religion. On August 10, 1680, thousands of people in more than two dozen Pueblos rose up and attacked their Spanish conquerors. By late August, the Spanish had fled from New Mexico. Spanish churches were destroyed. People returned to their old ways.

The Spanish did not return to New Mexico until 1692. This time, they were not so brutal. They allowed the Pueblo to follow a mix of Christianity and their **traditional** religions.

▲ Mission San Xavier del Bac near Tucson, Arizona, was built in the late 1700s. It is the most elaborately decorated Spanish mission in the Southwest.

Arizona missions

Meanwhile, a priest named Eusibio Kino was establishing **missions** in what is now southern Arizona. These missions were small communities where priests taught the Southwest Indians about Christianity and tried to get them to live more like Europeans. Kino treated the native people with more kindness than most Europeans in the region.

Still, many Southwest Indians resented the Spanish and their missions. They had their own religions, which they did not want to give up. They did not want to give up their traditional ways of life.

Apaches sometimes attacked the missions. The Tohono O'odham also revolted. They forced the Spanish to close some missions. By the 1820s, only two missions remained active in Arizona.

Deadly diseases

Diseases such as **measles** and **smallpox** had long been common in Europe. But American Indians had never been exposed to European diseases, so their bodies couldn't fight them. The diseases quickly raced through native villages, killing thousands.

▲ This drawing shows a Spanish attack on Pueblo Indians.

What Happened After the United States Took Over?

When the United States declared its independence from Great Britain in 1776, the **nation** consisted of 13 states along the East Coast. During the decades that followed, the nation grew, spreading across the continent. In 1846 the United States and Mexico went to war over land in Texas. Two years later, the United States won the war and forced Mexico to give up most of the land that is now the American Southwest. The Southwest Indians were suddenly living in a different nation.

Americans began moving in. White settlers streamed across Southwest Indian land. They killed **game** and used water that Southwest Indians needed. They settled on American Indian lands, starting farms and establishing mines.

▲ Apaches wait in line for food on the San Carlos **Reservation** in Arizona.

Many Southwest Indians fought against the intruders. Apaches began attacking wagon trains and settlements. They were not going to be pushed aside easily.

Reservations

To try to keep the peace, the U.S. government began establishing reservations. These lands were set aside solely for use by American Indians. The nation's first reservation in the southwest, the Gila River Indian Community, was established near present-day Phoenix, Arizona, in 1859.

Southwest Indians struggled to survive. They could not always find enough food on the reservations, but they were not supposed to hunt off the reservations. Food and other supplies that the government promised did not always arrive.

Many Apaches resisted living on reservations. Apache leaders such as Cochise, Victorio, and Geronimo led their people into the mountains of southern Arizona where the U.S. Army could not track them. Not until 1886 were all Apaches forced onto reservations.

BIOGRAPHY

Cochise: Apache Leader

Cochise was a fearless leader of the Chiricahua band of Apaches. When the government offered his people a reservation far from their homeland, he refused and led his people into the mountains. Later, the government agreed to give the Chiricahua Apache a reservation in their **traditional** lands. Until his death, Cochise worked to maintain peace between Apaches and their neighbors.

The long walk

Navajos also fought against the invasion of their land. The U.S. Army gave Colonel Kit Carson the task of defeating the Navajo. Carson and his men burnt Navajo crops, destroyed their homes, and shot any Navajo they saw. Finally, Navajos had no choice but to surrender.

The government assigned them land in southeastern New Mexico, far from their homes. In the winter of 1864, the surviving Navajos were forced to walk over 200 miles (320 kilometers) to reach this reservation. Hundreds died on the journey across the frigid land. To this day, Navajos look back in horror at what they call the "Long Walk."

The Navajo people spent four years on this miserable, barren reservation. Finally, they convinced the U.S. government to allow them to return to their traditional homeland in the **Four Corners** region.

▲ Resettled Navajos build living quarters with **adobe** brick after the "Long Walk."

The 1900s

In 1924 the United States finally gave American Indians U.S. citizenship. Native people in the Southwest were committed to their traditions and beliefs. Many also became committed to the United States.

During World War II, American Indians joined the military at a higher rate than any other group. One group of Navajos became extremely valuable to the war effort. They were known as the "code talkers." At the time, military commanders sent orders over the radio. They sent the messages in code, but these codes were often broken.

Around the world, only a handful of non-Navajos spoke the Navajo language. So Navajo soldiers created a code based on their own language. No one could understand the words, much less figure out the code. The Navajos' code was never broken.

◀ About 400 Navajos served as code talkers during World War II.

What Is Life Like Today for Southwest Indians?

Today large numbers of American Indians still make their homes in the Southwest. More than 300,000 American Indians live in Arizona. Another 200,000 live in New Mexico, about 9.7 percent of the state's total population. Only Alaska is home to a higher percentage of **descendants** of the first inhabitants of North America.

There are 43 different official American Indian **nations** in the Southwest. With more than 250,000 members, the Navajo nation is the largest. It also covers the greatest area, stretching across almost 27,000 acres (11,000 hectares) in the **Four Corners** region.

Each American Indian nation elects its own leaders. The nations have their own laws, their own police departments, and their own court systems. Members of each nation follow the laws of the United States, but they also follow the laws of their own nation.

▲ Kathy Kitcheyan, San Carlos Apache chairperson, testifies before Congress.

The nations also run their own schools. In these schools, children study their own language and culture along with standard school subjects. In 1968 the Navajos started Navajo Community College, the first college in the country run by an American Indian nation. The school is now known as Diné College. Its 2,000 students can attend college without having to leave the **reservation**.

Many American Indians in the Southwest live on reservations, while others live in towns and cities off the reservation. Regardless of where they live, they work in offices and banks, on farms and in laboratories. They are part of the larger American society, but many remain connected to the traditions and **customs** of their **ancestors**. They keep one foot placed firmly in each world.

◄ Teenagers play basketball on the Navajo Reservation.

Timeline

about 10,000 BCE   The first people arrive in North America.

1 CE   Mogollon, Hohokam, and Ancestral Puebloan cultures arise.

1200s   Ancestral Puebloans begin abandoning their cities.

1300s   Hohokam people leave their settlements.

1300s   Navajos and Apaches arrive in the Southwest.

1540   Francisco Vásquez de Coronado leads a Spanish **expedition** searching for gold in the Southwest.

1598   Juan de Oñate establishes a Spanish settlement in the land of the Pueblo people.

1680   The Pueblo people revolt against the Spanish, forcing them from New Mexico.

1691   Father Eusebio Kino begins establishing **missions** among American Indians in what is now Arizona.

1692   The Spanish regain control of New Mexico.

1848   At the end of the Mexican American War, the Southwest becomes U.S. territory.

1859   The Gila River Indian Community is established. It is the nation's first **reservation**.

1864   Hundreds of Navajos die on the "Long Walk," when they are forced to walk over 200 miles (320 kilometers) to a distant reservation.

1886   The last Apaches are moved onto reservations.

1924   American Indians become U.S. citizens.

1934   The Indian Reorganization Act returns American Indians' authority to self-govern and reverses some of the unfair government policies of the past.

1942-45   Navajo "code talkers" send important messages during World War II.

1968   The Navajo **Nation** establishes the first Native American college, today known as Diné College.

1968   The American Indian Movement (AIM) organizes protests against the unfair treatment of American Indians and calls on the government to keep its promises to the people.

1990   Congress passes the Native American Languages Act, "to **preserve**, protect, and promote the rights and freedoms of all Native Americans to use, practice and develop Native American languages."

1990   On August 3, President George H.W. Bush proclaims the first National American Indian Heritage Month. President Clinton affirms this special designation in November of 1996.

2004   The National Museum of the American Indian is established on the National Mall in Washington, D.C.

2010   More than half a million American Indians live in Arizona and New Mexico.

Glossary

adobe brick made of Sun-dried mud and clay

affiliation close connection, often as a member

ancestor family member from the distant past

archaeologist scientist who studies bones and items left behind by ancient people to learn about the past

Bering Strait narrow body of water that separates Russia from Alaska

custom usual practice of a group

descendant the children of an earlier group of people

drought period of little or no rainfall

expedition trip for the purpose of exploration

Four Corners region of the United States that spans northeastern Arizona, northwestern New Mexico, southwestern Colorado, and southeastern Utah

game animals that are hunted

gully trench worn in the earth by running water

hogan traditional Navajo house

kachina spirit in the Hopi or Pueblo religions; dancers embodying the spirits; dolls that represent the spirits

kilt knee-length skirt worn by men

kiva underground room where Hopis and Pueblos hold religious ceremonies

mammoth large extinct animal of the elephant family

measles disease marked by fever and red spots

mission place where people teach their religion to others

mortar building material that is spread between stones to hold them together

nation make sure to state this can be a "tribe" or a country, since the word is used both ways in the book

nomadic moving from place to place without a fixed home

plunder take goods by force

preserve protect from harm or ruin

reservation land set aside for American Indians to live on

smallpox deadly disease that causes fever and rash

spring source of water coming from the ground

traditional handed down from age to age

trait quality that sets one person or group apart from another

tribe group made up of many families that share the same language and customs

wickiup dome-shaped Indian shelter

Find Out More

Books

Croy, Anita. *National Geographic Investigates Ancient Pueblo: Archaeology Unlocks the Secrets of America's Past.* Washington, D.C.: National Geographic, 2007.

Holm, Tom. *Code Talkers and Warriors: Native Americans in World War II.* New York: Chelsea House, 2007.

Sonneborn, Liz. *The Apache.* New York: Franklin Watts, 2005.

St. Lawrence, Genevieve. *The Pueblo and Their History.* Minneapolis, Minn.: Compass Point, 2005.

Websites

Chaco Culture National Historic Park
www.nps.gov/chcu
Learn about the Chaco Culture National Historic Park at this site.

Indigenous Voices of the Colorado Plateau
http://library.nau.edu/speccoll/exhibits/indigenous_voices/
The Indigenous Voices of the Colorado Plateau page has information on many Southwest tribes.

National Museum of the American Indian
www.nmai.si.edu/education/codetalkers/
The National Museum of the American Indian has information on the important role American Indians played in World War II.

Native America in New Mexico
www.newmexico.org/nativeamerica/
Visit this page to discover more about the American Indians of New Mexico.

DVDs

In Search of History: Navajo Code Talkers. A&E Home Video, 2006.

In Search of History: Pueblo Cliffdwellers. A&E Home Video, 2006.

Places to visit

Acoma Pueblo
Acoma, NM
www.puebloofacoma.org/

Chaco Culture National Historical Park
www.nps.gov/chcu/index.htm
Nageezi, NM

Heard Museum
2301 N. Central Avenue
Phoenix, AZ
www.heard.org/

Further research

What was the most interesting topic you read about in this book? Would you like to learn more about how Pueblo people make pottery? Perhaps you would like to better understand the Spanish relationship with the American Indians. You can find out much more by visiting your local library or searching online.

Index